THE OFFICIAL
WEST BROMWICH
ANNUAL 2022

Written by Dave Bowler
Designed by Monika Krakowiak

A Grange Publication

A Grange Publication

© 2021. Published by Grange Communications Ltd., Edinburgh, under licence from West Bromwich Albion Football Club. Printed in the EU.

Every effort has been made to ensure the accuracy of information within this publication but the publishers cannot be held responsible for any errors or omissions. Views expressed are those of the author and do not necessarily represent those of the publishers or the football club. All rights reserved.

Photographs © West Bromwich Albion FC, AMA Photography & Laurie Rampling.

ISBN 978-1-913578-86-2

CONTENTS

LEADING FROM THE FRONT

Dealing with Albion's return to the Championship – and a hopeful elevation back to the Premier League – was placed in the hands of new head coach Valérien Ismaël when he took over at The Hawthorns in July 2021.

The 45-year-old began coaching at senior level in Germany in 2014 at FC Nuremberg and VfL Wolfsburg ahead of leading Austrian side LASK for the 2019/20 season.

They enjoyed a great Europa League run, winning a group containing Sporting Lisbon, PSV Eindhoven and Rosenborg before beating AZ Alkmaar in the knock-out phase and eventually losing to Manchester United.

He became boss at relegation-threatened Barnsley in October 2020 and took the team all the way to fifth place in the Championship last season, before they were beaten in the play-offs.

Arriving at The Hawthorns, he immediately set to work planning Albion's future.

"I feel really proud to have accepted this challenge and I'm ready to get to work.

"I feel a big responsibility but I'm ready for this job and I am delighted to be here.

"I know a lot about the club's history and the atmosphere at The Hawthorns, which is an amazing stadium, and the fans make it a special place to play.

"This was the next step I wanted to take in my career and I'm ready to work with everyone at this club. Although there's going to be a lot of hard work this season, I am excited for the big task in front of us.

"It's a big commitment from the club to want me to implement a philosophy I want for the next four years. My first task is to implement a new identity that the fans can enjoy and one where they can see the players are there for each other and give everything on the pitch to win games. We have a clear plan and vision of where we want to go.

"We're going to need everyone, especially our fans, to support the team. It's a new start for everyone and it's important that we take on this new challenge together, and we'll continue to work hard to make the fans proud this year.

"We are very happy with the group here and now it's about working on the motivation and mentality of the boys.

"We have the quality but the big difference in this division is the mentality you need. It's up to me and my staff to create the right mentality for the players and they need to quickly prepare for the Championship and be ready to compete."

Season Review

There has never been a season like 2020/21 — and let's hope there'll never be another season like it again. With almost all of it played out in front of empty stadia, it was a real reminder that without fans to support the players, the game is not the same.

The empty grounds were all because of the Covid pandemic of course, but that also meant that players and staff had to be especially careful to make sure they didn't test positive for the virus and leave themselves, and maybe some of their team-mates, having to self-isolate for a period.

On top of that, because the previous season had finished so late, it meant that 2020/21 kicked off a whole month later than usual which meant packing a nine month season into just eight, putting plenty of strain on the players as they had to battle through the workload.

None of that was ideal for a newly promoted team heading into the Premier League, particularly having to play home games without the backing of the crowd at The Hawthorns, but as ever, there was plenty of optimism at the start of the campaign, as Slaven Bilic's team started with a home game…

SEPTEMBER

Leicester City were the first opponents coming to The Hawthorns off the back of a strong season that had seen them qualify for Europe under Brendan Rodgers. The first half was promising enough for the Baggies but if you don't take your chances in the Premier League, it can be costly. That proved the case in the second half when Castagne gave the Foxes the lead before two late penalties from Vardy sewed up the points. Even so, there were encouraging signs.

The same was true of the first away trip, to Everton. Grady Diangana scored the season's first Albion goal to grab the lead after ten minutes but by half-time the game had turned around, Everton leading 2-1 and the Baggies down to ten men after Kieran Gibbs was sent off. Even then, Matheus Pereira levelled things up early in the second half but in the end, the extra man that Everton had made the difference as the Toffees won 5-2.

Either side of that game, Albion's League Cup campaign had started and finished, the Throstles seeing off Harrogate Town 3-0 at home, then welcoming Brentford the week after. That game ended at 2-2 before our visitors won the penalty shootout 5-4.

No matter. Albion ended the month on a high from a fantastic game with Chelsea. The Baggies were on fire in the first half, Callum Robinson scoring twice and Kyle Bartley getting another to make it 3-0 after 27 minutes. But Chelsea gradually clawed their way back into things in the second half and right at the death, Abraham made it 3-3. An epic game though!

OCTOBER

Albion hoped to build on that first league point a week later when they went to the south coast to play Southampton, but this time, things did not go their way as the Saints were in good form. The home side kept good possession of the ball and a goal either side of half-time from Djenepo and then Romeu proved too much for the Baggies to come back from.

It meant the home game with struggling Burnley was suddenly very important. Albion were a lot better than they had been at Southampton and they dominated the vast majority of the 90 minutes. Eleven shots, eight corners, 57% of the ball all showed just how superior Albion were, but could they get the ball in the Burnley net? No. Thankfully, neither could Burnley and it was another point from a 0-0 draw.

Another big game followed, the Baggies going back down to the seaside to visit Brighton, another team expected to be at the bottom end of the table. We actually had more possession than Brighton did but a Jake Livermore own goal just before half-time looked as if it would decide the game. Karlan Grant thought otherwise though and he popped up seven minutes from the end to give Albion a third draw in four games.

NOVEMBER

With Albion starting to get to grips with the Premier League, there were high hopes as we travelled down to our fellow newly promoted team Fulham. But it was to be an off-day for the Baggies with Fulham always looking more dangerous. They scored twice in four minutes just before the half hour mark and hard as Albion tried, there was really no way back after that.

Tottenham were the next visitors to The Hawthorns, sporting a forward line of Kane, Bale and Son, which is pretty frightening! But the Throstles defended determinedly, Sam Johnstone made some fine saves and it looked as if we would get ourselves another point. But then, two minutes from time, Harry Kane, who always seems to score against Albion, grabbed the winner.

The Premier League rarely gets any easier and it was off to Manchester United next – though Albion have had quite a good recent record at Old Trafford. They played really well again but it was a game of VAR controversy as United got the game's only goal through a Fernandes penalty that perhaps shouldn't have been given. Familiar story for Albion in the Premier League!

November ended on a high though as the Throstles registered a first league win of the season in game number ten. Sheffield United, suffering a poor start to the campaign, were the visitors and Albion simply had to win. So they did! Conor Gallagher's 13th minute goal was enough to separate the teams and give Albion real encouragement as we headed towards Christmas.

DECEMBER

Crystal Palace were next to come to The Hawthorns with former Baggies boss Roy Hodgson in charge. There were no favours from Roy though. It was 1-1 when, after 34 minutes, Matheus Pereira was red carded, to his obvious surprise! Hodgson made use of the interval to tell his players how to use the man over and Palace ripped through Albion in the second half, winning 5-1.

Another former Albion man bit us in the next game. Albion travelled to Newcastle and were well worth a draw, Darnell Furlong equalising Almiron's first minute opener. But with eight minutes left, Gayle won the game for the Magpies. Heartbreaking for the Albion.

To their credit, they responded brilliantly at Manchester City three days later, coming

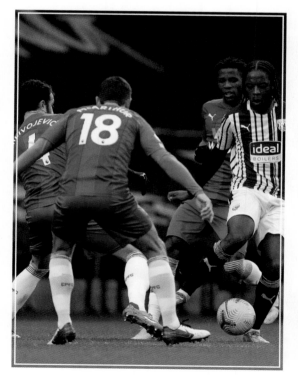

away from the Etihad with a 1-1 draw. But with Albion 19th in the table, with seven points from 13 games, the club decided it was time for a change of head coach. Out went Slaven Bilic and in his place came Sam Allardyce.

His first game was the local derby with Aston Villa at The Hawthorns. There was to be no fairy-tale start for Big Sam, Albion a goal down after five minutes and then went a man down half an hour later as Livermore got his marching orders. The Baggies were well organised in the second half but in the end, the Villa made the extra man count with two goals in the last five minutes.

It was up to Anfield next and across the first half, Albion were barely able to get out of their own half as Liverpool pounded forward and took a 1-0 lead after 12 minutes through Mané.

But just like the game at Manchester City, Albion battled and fought for every ball and with eight minutes to go, Semi Ajayi levelled things up. Albion might even have won the game, but with 22% possession, let's not be greedy!

Brilliantly as Albion had defended at Liverpool, those skills completely deserted them as the year came to a close with a visit from Leeds United. The team that won automatic promotion alongside the Baggies simply sliced us apart and were 4-0 ahead by half-time. Thankfully they only managed one more after the break, but it was a disappointing way to end a sad year for everyone.

JANUARY

The new year did not bring a change in fortunes either. Arsenal came to The Hawthorns having had a poor first half of the season but they found it just as easy to score goals as Crystal Palace and Leeds had in December. It was 4-0 to the Arsenal and to be honest, it might have been worse though this time, at least Albion had chances of our own.

The Baggies enjoy a penalty shootout about as much as the England team do and we were knocked out of the FA Cup by another after drawing 2-2 in the third round at Blackpool. They won the shootout 3-2.

A massive game followed, Albion travelling the short distance to Molineux to take on Wolves in the derby game. The last time we had been there, we had won 5-1 in 2012. Could we do it again? Not quite, but we did breathe some fresh life into our season with a fantastic 3-2 win. Pereira gave us a perfect start with an eighth minute penalty, but we were 2-1 down by the break. But the game wasn't over and after Ajayi scored an equaliser, a second Pereira penalty after 56 minutes tied up all three points.

A trip to West Ham was a tough assignment with David Moyes' side threatening to get in the Champions League places. They were just a shade too strong on the day, the Throstles far from disgraced as we slid to a 2-1 defeat in a game where we impressed.

We had the wind knocked out of our sails in the next game though. Title chasing Manchester City were in town and, mindful of the draw we had earned in December, there was no underestimating Albion this time as they swept to a 5-0 win.

With Fulham a side we needed to overtake if we were going to claw our way to Premier League safety, their visit to West Bromwich was a game we simply had to win. A goal behind at the interval, we had turned that around in the first 21 minutes of the second half thanks to strikes from Bartley and Pereira. But the Baggies couldn't hold on to the advantage and a 76th minute equaliser from Cavaleiro meant a draw that didn't really help either side.

FEBRUARY

February started with another must-win game and sadly, Albion didn't. They took the lead at Sheffield United through Matt Phillips just before half-time, but couldn't make the most of it and ended up losing the game 2-1. The Baggies were still 19th, but nine points from safety.

A first visit to Tottenham's new stadium followed and once again, the Throstles put in an excellent first half performance to reach the break at 0-0. But Kane and Son were at it again early in the second half and Albion simply couldn't handle them as Spurs won 2-0.

Albion were becoming much harder to break down and that was vital against Manchester United at The Hawthorns. After Albion scored through Mbaye Diagne after just two minutes, the visitors had 73% of the ball but rarely saw a sight of the Albion goal. Fernandes made the most of one of the few opportunities and earned his side a 1-1 draw.

Albion eked out another 0-0 draw at Turf Moor against Burnley, but by now, it was wins we were needing rather than gritty draws. One of those came at the end of the month as we hosted Brighton. Bartley scored an early goal and from there, it was all about "they shall not pass"! Determined, hard working and well organised, Albion kept a crucial clean sheet and won the game.

MARCH

It was something to build on in another home game, with Everton coming to The Hawthorns. There was nothing between the sides until after 65 minutes, Richarlison won the game.

Newcastle United were next to visit as Albion finished a run of three home games. They completed the full set of results too, a 0-0 draw not exactly getting the TV audience off their seats! It was further proof that Albion were becoming more competitive but the goals just would not come – not that VAR was doing much to help in that direction...

Albion headed into a three week break from action with the long trip to Selhurst Park. Once again, it was the same old story of Albion playing well, not quite being able to break down the opposition and being beaten by the only goal of the game, Milivojevic's 37th minute penalty. Things were looking bleak now.

APRIL

The visit to Stamford Bridge at the start of April was probably the game of the season from an Albion point of view – and this time it was us that had the extra man. Chelsea took the lead but then had Thiago Silva dismissed on the half hour. Two goals inside a minute from Pereira had Albion leading at the break, then Robinson and Diagne made it 4-1. Chelsea pulled one back before Robinson put the icing on the cake to make it 5-2.

Southampton were at The Hawthorns nine days later and you could see the confidence running through the Baggies. Pereira knocked in a penalty after 32 minutes, Phillips made it 2-0 three minutes later and the game was over, Robinson making it 3-0 in the second half. Six points out of six! Eight points from safety, seven to play. Was a great escape possible?

Leicester brought us down to earth with a 3-0 beating, all of the goals coming in the first half, but again the Throstles showed real character at Villa Park in the next game. Recovering from conceding a ninth minute penalty, Albion led 2-1 until time added on when Davis equalised. That was a hammer blow going into the final month of the campaign.

MAY

Another derby started May, Albion coming back from behind to ensure that Wolves hasn't beaten us at home

in the 21st century, but that was small consolation really. With four games left, we would have to win them all to have any chance of surviving.

A trip to Arsenal settled matters, a 3-1 defeat condemning the Baggies to relegation. Again, you couldn't fault the battling nature of the players in the game until Willian scored the Gunners' third in the last minute, but you need a bit more than that in the Premier League.

A bit of luck doesn't hurt either and Albion had none of that all season. Hosting Liverpool, Hal Robson-Kanu gave us an early lead which Salah wiped off on 33 minutes but going into six minutes of added time, we were still getting a creditable draw. And then Liverpool sent their goalkeeper up for a corner – and he scored. It was that kind of season…

We did at least welcome 5,371 Baggies fans back to The Hawthorns for the visit of West Ham and it was great to hear some noise in the old ground at last. Again, we started well and scored the first goal through Pereira but the season's major fault – conceding goals late in each half – came back to haunt us as the Hammers went away with a 3-1 win.

The season came to an end with a trip to Leeds and just as they had at The Hawthorns, they blew us away again, 3-0 up before Robson-Kanu got the consolation of the season's last goal.

It wasn't the season we wanted but the great thing about football is there's always next season to look forward to!

WEST BROMWICH ALBION
2020/21

WEST BROMWICH ALBION 2020/21

Date	Opponent	Score	Scorers	Year
Sep 13	Leicester City (H)	0-3		
Sep 20	Harrogate (EFL Cup1) (H)	3-0	Harper, Robson-Kanu, Robinson	
Sep 19	Everton (A)	2-3	Diangana, Pereira	
Sep 22	Brentford (EFL Cup 2) (H) (Brentford won 5-4 on penalties)	2-2	Robson-Kanu (2 pens)	
Sep 26	Chelsea (H)	3-3	Robinson (2), Bartley	
Oct 4	Southampton (A)	0-2		
Oct 19	Burnley (H)	0-0		
Oct 26	Brighton & Hove Albion (A)	1-1	Grant	
Nov 2	Fulham (A)	0-2		
Nov 8	Tottenham Hotspur (H)	0-1		2020
Nov 21	Manchester United (A)	0-2		
Nov 28	Sheffield United (H)	1-0	Gallagher	
Dec 6	Crystal Palace (H)	1-5	Gallagher	
Dec 12	Newcastle United (A)	1-2	Furlong	
Dec 15	Manchester City (A)	1-1	Dias (og)	
Dec 20	Aston Villa (H)	0-3		
Dec 27	Liverpool (A)	1-1	Ajayi	
Dec 29	Leeds United (H)	0-5		
Jan 2	Arsenal (H)	0-4		
Jan 9	Blackpool (FA Cup 3) (A (Blackpool won 3-2 on penalties)	2-2	Ajayi, Pereira (pen)	
Jan 16	Wolverhampton Wanderers (A)	3-2	Pereira (2 pens), Ajayi	
Jan 19	West Ham United (A)	1-2	Pereira	
Jan 26	Manchester City (H)	0-5		
Jan 30	Fulham (H)	2-2	Bartley, Pereira	
Feb 2	Sheffield United (A)	1-2	Phillips	
Feb 7	Tottenham Hotspur (A)	0-2		
Feb 14	Manchester United (H)	1-1	Diagne	
Feb 20	Burnley (A)	0-0		
Feb 27	Brighton & Hove Albion (H)	1-0	Bartley	2021
Mar 04	Everton (H)	0-1		
Mar 13	Crystal Palace (A)	0-1		
Apr 3	Chelsea (A)	5-2	Pereira (2), Robinson (2), Diagne	
Apr 12	Southampton (H)	3-0	Pereira (pen), Phillips, Robinson	
Apr 22	Leicester City (A)	0-3		
Apr 25	Aston Villa (A)	2-2	Pereira (pen), Mings (og)	
May 3	Wolverhampton Wanderers (H)	1-1	Diagne	
May 9	Arsenal (A)	1-3	Pereira	
May 16	Liverpool (H)	1-2	Robson-Kanu	
May 19	West Ham United (H)	1-3	Pereira	
May 23	Leeds United (A)	1-3	Robson-Kanu	

LOST IN WEST BROMWICH!

New Albion boss Valérian Ismaël has found his way to Halfords Lane and The Hawthorns, but it looks like he's going to need some assistance in finding his way back to the training ground.

Is it you that he's calling? If it is, you'd better be ready to help him through the maze…

(Answer on page 61)

THE HAWTHORNS

TRAINING GROUND

ALEX OF THE ALBION

Valérien Ismaël didn't hang about once he'd taken over as Albion's head coach. Almost immediately, he signed up midfielder Alex Mowatt from his former club, Barnsley.

He was Barnsley captain last term, scoring eight goals and registering seven assists as the Tykes reached the Championship play-offs. But when he was given the chance to link up with his former boss, he was only too pleased to come to The Hawthorns.

"I wanted to get the deal done as quickly as possible once I heard about Albion's interest. I came for my medical and had a look around and I really liked the place.

"I played under the gaffer at Barnsley last season so that helps in terms of settling in. We have a really good relationship. He's one of those people who demands 100 per cent every day, which is what I do anyway.

"We get on really well and we talk a lot. When he came here and after I heard there was interest in me from the club, I just wanted to get it done.

"His pressing is intense. I think the fans will like that. You get after the ball and you play high up the pitch.

"I think the lads will really like the way he is every day on the training pitch.

"I'm confident I can perform here. I had a good season last year at Barnsley, scoring a few goals and getting a handful of assists too.

"I like to score goals from midfield, have plenty of shots and try and be as creative as possible.

"It's massive for me that the club wants to get back to the Premier League. It's an exciting challenge to be part of.

"I've always wanted to play in the Premier League, so to come to a club who have been in the Premier League plenty of times is really important for me.

"Everyone wants to aim for the same thing and that's promotion.

"I've never been promoted to the Premier League before and that's the best thing that could happen this season."

LAUNDRY DISASTER!

Conor Townsend took his Albion kit to the laundry and look what happened - all the colour washed out of everything!

Can you give him a hand and put the colours back?

It can be this season's kit, an away kit or a completely new design – the choice is yours!

Callum Robinson

FROM ALBION TO ALBION!

Albion added to their defensive strength for 2021/22 with the arrival of centre-half Matt Clarke on loan from the other Albion – Brighton.

Matt knows his way around the Championship having spent the two previous seasons on loan at Derby County. He has made 77 Championship appearances over the course of the last two years and says his sights are set on helping Albion mount a promotion push.

"I'd like to think I am someone who sets myself high standards and tries to keep to them throughout the whole season. I want to be able to give my best to West Bromwich Albion.

"As a player, you play football to achieve success. This is a club which is looking to bounce straight back to the Premier League and has had success at this level before.

"The club knows what it takes to get out of this division and I want to try and help them do it again this year.

"I think you need a bit of everything to get out of this league. You obviously need quality, but you also need to be a team and dig in. It's a tough league, but you have to relish the challenge and look forward to it.

"As soon as I heard Albion were interested in me, that was the option I wanted to pursue. I met the manager and he spoke about his philosophy and what he wants to do and where I might fit into all that.

"Everyone has to be pushing each other if you want to win promotion. You can't afford to take your foot off the gas.

"If everyone is working towards the same goal then the team is going to be a lot stronger for it.

"I really hope I can do well here and the target this season has to be promotion."

Goals, Goals, Goals!

Can you find the names of the last ten men to finish the season as Albion's top goalscorer in the table below?

Find the words in the grid. Words can go horizontally, vertically and diagonally in all eight directions.

```
P R R O D R I G U E Z J
B O B D K J G P G O L U
L N F L M G F Z D Z N H
T D Q W B J A E M A F W
T O L R Z U M Y K F B X
J N X D N W K N L E N A
A U S T I N O A R E B R
R W N N B S Z A K B L I
C F G T B H H L L U T E
T I D O N I X R J L L R
E C R G N B H Z Y W B E
Y M N O N G E S S E S P
```

Just to help you, they are:

Pereira Robson-Kanu Austin Gayle Rondon
Rodriguez Berahino Sessegnon
Lukaku Odemwingie

(Answers on page 61)

ALBION'S 11 !

At the end of the 2020/21 season, Chris Brunt announced that he was hanging up his boots for the final time.

The future will feature him returning to The Hawthorns as a coach with the Albion Academy – so the left side of the team should be fine for years ahead!

Brunty has made perhaps the biggest contribution to the Albion in the 21st century to date, so we thought we should show you all the facts and figures of one of the great Albion careers!

SIGNED: 15 AUGUST 2007
DEBUT: 1 SEPTEMBER 2007

421	Albion appearances
352	starts
69	substitute appearances
13th	in the all-time Albion list
382	league games
320	starts
62	substitute appearances
269	Premier League games
237	starts
32	substitute appearances
113	Championship games
83	starts
30	substitute appearances
28	FA Cup games
22	starts
6	substitute appearances

9	League Cup games
8	starts
1	substitute appearance
49	international caps for Northern Ireland - a club record
49	Premier League assists
47	Albion goals
24	Premier League goals
19	Championship goals
2	FA Cup goals
2	League Cup goals
6	headers
3	right foot
38	left foot
4	penalties
8	free-kicks
16	from outside the box
31	inside the box
9	inside the six yard box

Football moves fast these days and it's no different in the women's game as its development outpaces any other part of the sport.

That's certainly the case with West Bromwich Albion Women's Football Club, where it's all change in 2021 with a new manager, coaches, players and Chair in place.

After a successful settling period in the FA Women's National League Northern Premier Division over the past two seasons, the club is looking for a fresh promotion push in the coming seasons.

Jenny Sugarman is the new first team manager, replacing the outgoing Louis Sowe. She has two decades' worth of experience in the women's game having previously coached at Aston Villa and managed Loughborough Foxes.

Such is the increasing draw of the women's game's development, new coaching pathways are being opened up across the higher leagues, giving greater opportunities for coaches, as well as supporting player development with ideas flowing between the men's and women's teams.

Darren Carter, a former Albion player, has joined Sugarman to progress his own coaching career and will add a rich playing experience of his own to the group.

Having been third at the point the 2020/21 season was curtailed through Covid, Albion have strengthened their ranks with six summer signings winging their way into Coles Lane, the Sutton Coldfield base.

Winger Janelle Straker joined from Solihull Moors, former Stoke forward Ashley Hayes arrived from Fylde, whilst full-back Ashlee Brown completes a tour of the Midlands, having previously turned out for Birmingham City, Aston Villa and Coventry United. Brown started her career as an Under-12 at the Albion's Centre of Excellence.

Portia-Milan Langley Wright and Anae Roberts - who both scored on their pre-season debuts against Cheltenham Town - and Alanna Chimonas make up the six new faces and bolster Albion's ranks for what promises to be a very competitive season.

REACH FOR THE SKY!

Adam Reach became another of Albion's summer intake when he joined from Sheffield Wednesday in July – and he came with a ringing endorsement from Baggies boss Valérian Ismaël.

"We recognised straight away that he was one of the players who were able to adapt to the intensity of play. He has big quality on the left side, a great mentality and is very dangerous with his crosses. He has the attributes we need – the mentality, the philosophy, the press and a never-give-up attitude.

"It's important that we have a player who knows the league and knows exactly what's going on. It will be a long, long, long season and it's important to have players who know exactly what they have to do."

Adam added to that by saying, "My main attributes are effort and determination. Every professional has to have that, of course, but I have plenty of it.

"I try and play at a high intensity. I try to be as positive as I can in terms of scoring goals and assisting goals.

"I try to play with a smile on my face and every so often if I can hit one into the top corner from 35 yards and send the fans home happy, then that's my job and that's what I want to do.

"I think the high intensity and the high press in this 3-4-3 formation is really coming into the game. You're seeing plenty of Premier League teams playing that way. I'd love to play that way.

"It's what I want to do and I think my physical attributes allow me to work hard and work at a high intensity throughout the game. Physically, I am ready to do that and mentally I am looking forward to learning the manager's style.

"I know that the manager is going to demand a lot from me physically, but I'm really excited for that. It's definitely going to be the biggest challenge of my career, but it's also the most exciting one.

"I'm just really excited to be here.

"It's a massive opportunity to come and play for a really, really big club which has aspirations to get back to the Premier League. That's where I want to be. It's always been my goal to get to the Premier League. Every player wants to play at the top level and I am certainly no different.

"I think I have the quality to play at the top end of this division, and hopefully the next division above too.

"Promotion has to be the aim for us. That's what I want to achieve here this season."

ALBION - FROM A to Z

ASTLE

The King, the charismatic Jeff Astle was the idol of the fans through the 1960s and into the 1970s, wearing number 9 and topping the scoring charts year after year. The Astle Gates at The Hawthorns were erected in his memory.

BOMBER

The nickname given to Tony Brown, the man who owns virtually every Albion record, be it games played or goals scored. Albion through and through, still covering games for the BBC, he has his own statue at The Hawthorns. Why not – it's his ground!

CYRILLE

You only need to say "Cyrille" for everyone to know who you are talking about – Cyrille Regis, perhaps the best loved footballer Albion have ever had. Goalscorer supreme, fighter against racism, superhero without a cape. There was only one Cyrille Regis.

DEFEATS

Albion's worst ever run of defeats came in the 1995/96 season when, under Alan Buckley, they lost 11 league games in a row. Even so, they still managed to finish in 11th place in the second tier, so they did pretty well otherwise!

EAST STAND

The East Stand is the newest part of The Hawthorns, opened at the beginning of the 2001/02 season after being built on the site of the old Rainbow Stand. It also houses club office, ticket office, club shop and hospitality facilities.

FA CUP

The Throstles have won the FA Cup on five separate occasions, which puts them joint tenth on the all-time list. Those wins came in 1888, 1892, 1931, 1954 and 1968 – maybe it's time to add another one!

GOALS

Albion's record goalscorer is Tony Brown with 281 goals in 735 games for the club. At the start of the 2021/22 season, Albion had scored 7,415 league goals and conceded 7,116. The club's first league goal was scored by Joe Wilson in 1888.

HAWTHORNS

The Hawthorns has been Albion's home since September 1900 when the first game ended in a 1-1 draw with Derby County. In total, before this season, Albion have played 2,285 league games there, winning 1,135, losing 578, scoring 4,169 goals and conceding 2,688.

ISMAËL

New head coach Valérian Ismaël joined the club in the summer of 2021, leaving Barnsley to take up the reins at The Hawthorns. He is hoping to become the fifth Albion manager to win promotion to the Premier League after Gary Megson, Tony Mowbray, Roberto di Matteo and Slaven Bilic.

JONAS

Jonas Olsson became a real cult hero at The Hawthorns after Tony Mowbray signed him from NEC Nijmegen in August 2008. The giant Swede played 261 times for the Albion over the next eight years and made his name as a ferocious competitor who wasn't frightened of any opponent – plenty were frightened of him!

KENNINGTON OVAL

Albion's first four FA Cup finals were all played at the Kennington Oval in London. They lost to Blackburn Rovers in 1886, Aston Villa in 1887, then beat Preston North End in 1888 and Villa in 1892. You are probably more used to seeing England and Surrey play cricket there now.

LEAGUE CUP

Albion didn't enter the League Cup in the first five seasons of its existence but when we did, it was with a bang. The Baggies won the cup first time out in 1965/66 and were losing finalists in 1967 and again in 1970.

MANAGERS

Albion have got through plenty of managers and head coaches over the years, with Valérian Ismaël becoming the 33rd permanent leader of the team since Albion first appointed a manager, Jack Smith, in 1948. Vic Buckingham had 267 games as boss, Pepe Mel just 17.

Northern Ireland

Northern Ireland has provided Albion with plenty of good players over the years, but especially in the 2010s when we were able to field Chris Brunt, Gareth McAuley and Jonny Evans in our team. The last two went to the Euros in 2016 but Brunt missed out with a knee injury.

Odemwingie

Peter Odemwingie was a huge hit for the Albion after Roberto di Matteo brought him to the club at the start of the 2010/11 Premier League season. He scored 31 goals in 90 Albion appearances, most famous among them a hat-trick at Molineux in 2012 as the Throstles beat Wolves 5-1.

Pennington

Jesse "Peerless" Pennington was one of the great early heroes of the football club, captaining the team to the Division One title in 1919/20 as well as winning 25 England caps, still the most any player has ever won at the Albion.

Queen Mother

Albion have never been presented with a trophy by the monarch of the day, but the closest we came was in 1954 when, after beating Preston North End 3-2 at Wembley, we were presented with the FA Cup by Queen Elizabeth, the Queen Mother.

Robson

Which Robson do you want?!? Bobby Robson, later the England manager, played 257 games, scoring 61 goals for the Throstles between 1956 and 1962. Later on, his Captain Marvel, Bryan Robson, started his career at The Hawthorns, playing 259 games and scoring 46 goals before leaving for Manchester United, then returning as manager. Bryan's brother Gary then played 256 games and scored 34 goals for the club.

Stoney Lane

Albion's home prior to the move to The Hawthorns, the 15 years at Stoney Lane from 1885 to 1900 saw the club become a power in the land, winning the FA Cup twice, reaching two more finals and becoming founder members of the Football League in 1888.

Taylor

"Super Bob" Taylor was the great goalscoring hero of the 1990s, not only firing the Throstles to promotion in 1993 but returning for a second spell at the club to score the crucial goals that secured a first ever promotion to the Premier League in 2002.

UNDERDOGS

Albion have a proud FA Cup history, but from time to time, they've been beaten by the underdog. Probably the worst example came in January 1991 when non-league Woking came to The Hawthorns for a third round FA Cup tie and won 4-2, Tim Buzaglo scoring a hat-trick for the visitors.

VALENCIA

Albion haven't had too many famous European nights but the greatest came on December 6 1978 when Valencia, favourites to win the UEFA Cup, came to town, bringing World Cup winner Mario Kempes with them. The tie was balanced at 1-1 from the first leg but Albion went on to win 2-0, both goals from Tony Brown.

WEMBLEY STADIUM

The old Wembley was a much happier venue for the Baggies who won four out of six games there – FA Cup finals in 1931, 1954 and 1968, as well as the play-off final in 1993 – losing just the 1935 FA Cup final and 1967 and 1970 League Cup finals. At the new Wembley, Albion lost in the play-off final in 2007 and the FA Cup semi-final in 2008.

XTRA-TIME

Albion's last FA Cup win saw us going all the way to extra-time before we managed to beat Everton 1-0 at Wembley in 1968. The winner came just three minutes into the extra period, Jeff Astle smashing a shot into the top corner from the edge of the box to win the game.

YELLOW & GREEN

Albion's best-known away kit, the yellow and green stripes were first worn in 1975/76 and they have become associated with good times and, especially, promotion seasons ever since. They were worn regularly in 1975/76, 1992/93, 2001/02, 2003/04 and 2019/20 as Albion went up a division and in the famous 1978/79 campaign.

ZOLTAN

Zoltan Gera, the Baggies' own magical Magyar, become a real fans' favourite during his two spells with the football club. Playing out wide, Gera specialised in scoring spectacular goals in big games and then celebrating with a somersault!

HUGILL OF THE HAWTHORNS!

Albion added to their attacking strength by signing Jordan Hugill from Norwich City on a season long loan just before the transfer window closed.

The 29-year-old played 31 times in the league for the Canaries in 2020/21, helping them to the Championship title and boss Valérien Ismaël is delighted to have him on board.

"Jordan is the type of striker we needed. He will suit us perfectly. He was immediately committed to Albion and to our way. I also think this is the right place for him.

"Jordan will allow us to be more adaptable as a team. We will have some games when we will need more physicality in the box, making life difficult for the opponent's centre-backs.

"He will help us link-up play and he will give us a different style, which is important in the Championship. He is strong in the air which will help us and he has a presence to win important duels.

"His skill and his experience will help him to score a lot of goals for us. He is able to score from open play and set-pieces. I think we saw already in our first few games that we have had a lot of crosses into the box and it is important we have a striker in the area who is able to win those headers."

Jordan was equally pleased to be at The Hawthorns.

"Coming here was the best option I could have possibly picked. You look at the size of the club and everything else that comes with the name West Bromwich Albion, it was something I just felt I had to be a part of.

"You look at the players in the squad and there's so much talent and experience. I'm really looking forward to being part of this team.

"You've got to have competition in a changing room. If you don't have competition then you don't have anything to push you to do better. I personally believe competition brings the best out in people and it certainly brings the best out in me.

"If you want to be a successful team then having competition for places is crucial. There are plenty of attacking players here with plenty of quality so I know I'll need to work hard to force my way into the team."

Dara O'Shea

WEST BROMWICH
ALBION

Getting Down to Business...

If you want to enjoy success, then you have to put the work in before you get the rewards.

That's true of anything you want to do in life, but especially when it comes to football.

With Albion looking for an immediate return to the Premier League, and with new manager Valérian Ismaël demanding an exciting, high energy style of play, then the players are going to have to work harder than ever to achieve their goal – and score their goals!

So back to work boys, no slacking!

SPOT THE BALL!

There was plenty of goalmouth action when Albion went to Leicester City last season but where's the ball gone?

Did Semi Ajayi or Kyle Bartley get their head on it? Did Schmeichel punch it clear? Did they all miss it?

Which one do you think is the real ball? _____

(Answer on page 61)

GOAL OF THE SEASON!

Callum Robinson certainly enjoyed coming up against Chelsea last season, scoring four goals across the two games as the European champions couldn't find a way to beat the Baggies.

Callum scored twice in the 3-3 draw at The Hawthorns early on in the season but unbelievably, there was better to come when Albion headed for Stamford Bridge later in the campaign.

Albion produced an incredible 5-2 win at the home of the Blues and Callum scored twice more.

Better yet, his first goal, a fierce volley that flashed into the roof of the net, was the winner of the Albion's goal of the season competition, despite fierce competition.

Congratulations Callum!

WHERE iN THE WORLD?

They say the world is getting smaller all the time and, as far as football goes, that may be true.

When Albion formed in 1878, the team was made up entirely of local lads. Then we started recruiting players from across other parts of the midlands, then England, then the rest of the UK and Ireland.

Nowadays, players come from all over the world to play for the Albion – so let's see just who has put West Bromwich Albion on the map back in their own country, shall we?

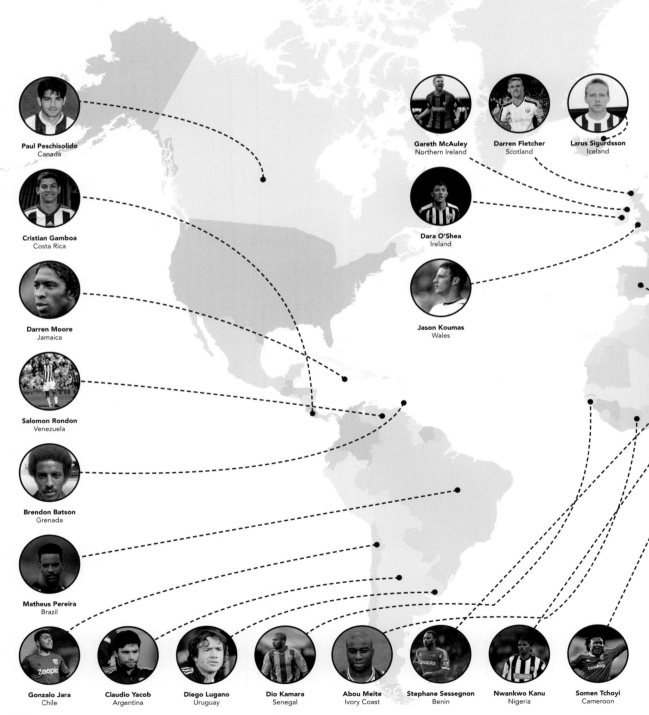

Paul Peschisolido
Canada

Cristian Gamboa
Costa Rica

Darren Moore
Jamaica

Salomon Rondon
Venezuela

Brendon Batson
Grenada

Matheus Pereira
Brazil

Gareth McAuley
Northern Ireland

Darren Fletcher
Scotland

Larus Sigurdsson
Iceland

Dara O'Shea
Ireland

Jason Koumas
Wales

Gonzalo Jara
Chile

Claudio Yacob
Argentina

Diego Lugano
Uruguay

Dio Kamara
Senegal

Abou Meite
Ivory Coast

Stephane Sessegnon
Benin

Nwankwo Kanu
Nigeria

Somen Tchoyi
Cameroon

Richard Sneekes
Netherlands

Thomas Gaardsoe
Denmark

Jonas Olsson
Sweden

Bernt Haas
Switzerland

Paul Scharner
Austria

Romelu Lukaku
Belgium

Filip Krovinovic
Croatia

Roman Bednar
Czechia

Serge Gnabry
Germany

Zoltan Gera
Hungary

Tomasz Kuszczak
Poland

Gabriel Tamas
Romania

Igor Balis
Slovakia

Robert Koren
Slovenia

Junichi Inamoto
Japan

Kim Do-Heon
South Korea

Youssouf Mulumbu
DR Congo

John Paskin
South Africa

Ahmed Hegazi
Egypt

Borja Valero
Spain

Artim Sakiri
Macedonia

Enzo Maresca
Italy

Jason Van Blerk
Australia

Chris Wood
New Zealand

BUILD AROUND BARTLEY!

Like Albion's team, we have Kyle Bartley in the middle here, but can you fill in all the blanks around him to complete this Baggies quiz?

(Answers on page 61)

1 – Romelu, Belgian international who had a season loan with Albion.
2 – Not the white stripes, the other colour!
3 – _____ Ismaël - the man in charge!
4 – How many times have Albion won the FA Cup?
5 – Albion's greatest goalscorer – he's got his own statue!
6 – Our home soil.
7 – Mr Diangana – what's his first name?
8 – The bird on the badge!
9 – Graham _____ - our latest cup winning captain.
10 – Our new signing from Barnsley.
11 – Romaine _____, our midfield man who's out on loan this season.

42

DARNELL FURLONG

ALBION AT THE WORLD CUP

The Euros are a fading memory now but never fear, the World Cup is just around the corner – it kicks off in Qatar on **21st November 2022**, so be prepared!

Albion men have played their part at World Cups in the past, going all the way back to 1958 when three Albion men wore the three lions in the tournament in Sweden.

Centre-forward Derek Kevan, right-back Don Howe and inside-forward Bobby Robson all played there, Don and Derek playing in all four of England's games, Bobby playing three. Derek was England's top scorer in the competition, with two of the four goals.

Albion were represented in Wales' team too, left-back Stuart Williams helping his side get all the way to the quarter-finals where they were beaten by a teenager making his first real mark on the competition – Pele of Brazil.

Twelve years later, in **1970**, Jeff Astle was on the plane to Mexico, and playing his part at centre-forward for England. He came on as a substitute against Brazil and then played from the start against Czechoslovakia as England reached the quarter-finals before losing out to West Germany.

It was Scotland who were the UK's representatives in **1978** and flying winger Willie Johnston was a dangerman in their team. He played just the once, in the 3-1 defeat to Peru, before he was on his way home after a hay fever remedy he was taking was found to be on the banned substances list.

Jimmy Nicholl completed the clean sweep of the UK countries when the Albion right-back was in the Northern Ireland squad for the **1986 World Cup in Mexico**. He played in all three group games as Northern Ireland were put out of the competition by Spain and Brazil.

It was 20 years before another Albion man played at the greatest show on earth, when it was the turn of Junichi Inamoto to figure for his country, starting one game and coming on as a sub in another as Japan fell at the first hurdle.

When the **World Cup went to South Africa in 2010**, there were a glut of Throstles at the tournament that followed our promotion back to the Premier League. Robert Koren captained Slovenia, played in all their three games and scored their first World Cup goal as they beat Algeria 1-0. Gonzalo Jara started three games and came on as a sub in the other as Chile made it to the last 16 before losing to Brazil.

Slovakia's Marek Cech played in their opening game, a 1-1 draw with a New Zealand side that featured Chris Wood. Wood came on as a sub in all three of New Zealand's games as they narrowly missed out on making progress to the knock-out games.

Four years on and in the Brazilian World Cup, England had its first Albion man in 44 years as goalkeeper Ben Foster kept a clean sheet in the group game against Costa Rica. Diego Lugano was also at the competition, captaining Uruguay in their first game. He picked up an injury in that game and that was his World Cup finished.

And so to **2018**, when Albion had two representatives in Russia. Ahmed Hegazi was in the Egyptian defence for all three of their games as they went out in the group stages, but Nacer Chadli enjoyed a longer stay in the tournament as Belgium finished third. He started four games, came on twice as a sub and scored a last-minute winner against Japan in the round of 16.

Can any Albion men better that in Qatar? Wait and see!

THE BIG QUIZ

1. Which club did Matt Clarke join Albion from? _____

2. And where did Kieran Gibbs go to? _____

3. How many England caps has Jake Livermore won? _____

4. Which country does Jayson Molumby play for? _____

5. In which country was Valérian Ismaël born? _____

6. Who scored Albion's first league goal of the 2020/21 season? _____

7. And who scored the last? _____

8. Who was Albion's most recent England goalkeeper _____
   before Sam Johnstone?

9. How many ex-Albion players have managed England? _____

10. When did Albion last win the FA Cup?

11. Who were Albion's first opponents in European competition?

12. And who were the most recent?

13. What was the original name of the club?

14. At the start of 2021/22, had Matt Phillips played 132, 172 or 202 games for the club?

15. Which club did we sign Karlan Grant from?

16. Where did Albion play before moving to The Hawthorns?

17. Who beat Albion in the FA Cup in 2020/21?

18. At which local club did Callum Robinson begin his career?

19. The 5-2 win at Stamford Bridge in April 2021 was the first time Albion have won at Chelsea in the Premier League – true or false?

20. Who has played the most games for the club?

US & Them

Some 23 teams stand between the Albion and a successful 2021/22 campaign – so let's take a look at how we have fared against them all in the league over the years!

BARNSLEY
P64 W23 D23 L18

Record win	7-0 (1989/90, 2006/07)
Record defeat	2-5 (1946/47)

BIRMINGHAM CITY
P120 W51 D35 L34

Record win	7-1 (1959/60)
Record defeat	0-4 (1947/48, 1998/99, 2004/05)

BLACKBURN ROVERS
P116 W41 D28 L47

Record win	8-1 (1935/36)
Record defeat	2-6 (1888/89)

BLACKPOOL
P80 W38 D12 L30

Record win	7-1 (1961/62)
Record defeat	1-5 (1955/56)

BOURNEMOUTH
P16 W6 D4 L6

Record win	4-0 (1991/92))
Record defeat	2-3 (1987/88)

BRISTOL CITY
P44 W19 D12 L13

Record win	4-1 (2007/08, 2009/10, 2019/20)
Record defeat	1-3 (1905/06, 1977/78)

CARDIFF CITY
P50 W21 D13 L16

Record win	6-1 (1953/54)
Record defeat	2-4 (1923/24)

COVENTRY CITY
P50 W24 D12 L14

Record win	7-1 (1978/79)
Record defeat	2-4 (1967/68, 2007/08)

DERBY COUNTY
P104 W35 D29 L40

Record win	5-0 (1888/89)
Record defeat	3-9 (1934/35)

FULHAM
P76 W31 D20 L25

Record win	6-1 (1946/47, 1962/63)
Record defeat	1-6 (2005/06)

HUDDERSFIELD TOWN
P70 W25 D16 L29

Record win	5-1 (1937/38)
Record defeat	1-5 (1920/21)

HULL CITY

P54 W21 D16 L17	
Record win	7-1 (1929/30)
Record defeat	1-5 (1909/10)

LUTON TOWN

P40 W22 D8 L10	
Record win	4-0 (1956/57, 1959/60, 1984/85)
Record defeat	1-5 (1957/58)

MIDDLESBROUGH

P92 W32 D21 L39	
Record win	6-3 (1934/35)
Record defeat	0-4 (1973/74, 2004/05)

MILLWALL

P36 W12 D10 L14	
Record win	6-1 (1929/30)
Record defeat	1-4 (1987/88, 1990/91)

NOTTINGHAM FOREST

P118 W52 D26 L40	
Record win	8-0 (1899/1900)
Record defeat	1-6 (1899/1900, 1900/01)

PETERBOROUGH UNITED

P6 W4 D1 L1	
Record win	4-0 (1991/92)
Record defeat	0-2 (1993/94)

PRESTON NORTH END

P102 W41 D24 L37	
Record win	4-0 (1959/60)
Record defeat	0-5 (1888/89, 1889/90, 1894/5)

QPR

P42 W19 D10 L13	
Record win	7-1 (2018/19)
Record defeat	1-4 (2014/15)

READING

P34 W19 D8 L7	
Record win	5-0 (1928/29)
Record defeat	3-5 (1928/29)

SHEFFIELD UNITED

P108 W41 D25 L42	
Record win	4-0 (1922/23, 1987/88)
Record defeat	0-6 (1999/2000)

STOKE CITY

P142 W46 D35 L61	
Record win	6-0 (1988/89)
Record defeat	3-10 (1936/37)

SWANSEA CITY

P42 W16 D9 L17	
Record win	6-2 (1929/30)
Record defeat	1-6 (1928/29)

21st Century Skippers

Plenty of men have worn the Albion armband since the turn of the century, so see if you can find some of them in this tricky crossword.

www.CrosswordWeaver.com

ACROSS

2 England goalkeeper, was in the Manchester City squad last season (surname) (6)

3 Sean, the skipper signed from Preston by Gary Megson (6)

5 Signed for us from Luton, became our record sale when he went to the Villa (first name) (6)

6 Mr Livermore! (4)

8 Brought in from Manchester United, Northern Ireland international (5,5)

9 Scottish international, installed as skipper by Tony Pulis (surname) (8)

DOWN

1 Giant centre-half who later returned to the club as head coach (surname) (5)

2 Two spells as Albion skipper for the number 11 with the wonderful left foot (5,5)

4 Midfield maestro who led us to the Championship title in 2008 (surname) (8)

5 Kevin _____ who joined us from Everton and helped us to the "great escape" (8)

7 Captained Albion to the first Premier League promotion (first name) (5)

MOLUMBY - THE MAN IN THE MIDDLE

Having already signed Matt Clarke, Albion returned to Brighton at the end of the summer transfer window to bring in 22-year-old midfielder Jayson Molumby on a season long loan, with a view to a permanent deal.

Albion boss Valérien Ismaël said, "Jayson is the perfect example of a player who has the right mentality and suits our philosophy. He is the right player for us and we are delighted to have him.

"His skills out of possession are incredible and he gives us more volume and more possibilities in midfield, which will support us with our intensity and this is one of his strengths."

Irish international Jayson was equally pleased to sign up at The Hawthorns.

"It's a massive club and I'm delighted to be here. I took my time in the window to decide where I wanted to be, so I was absolutely delighted when a club of Albion's size came in for me.

"One of the main reasons I jumped at the offer was the fact the club is trying to get out of the Championship and into the Premier League. As a footballer you want to be part of something successful and I'm confident I can achieve success here.

"I'm athletic. I'm a midfielder who likes to get around the pitch and be quite aggressive when needed. I've been trying to establish myself. I feel like I'm ready to settle at a club and be a key member of the team. I'm confident I can do that here."

PLAYER PROFILES

SAM JOHNSTONE

BIRTHDATE:	25 March 1993
POSITION:	Goalkeeper
HEIGHT:	1.79m
OTHER CLUBS:	Manchester United, Oldham, Scunthorpe, Walsall, Yeovil, Scunthorpe, Aston Villa
ALBION GAMES:	131
ALBION GOALS:	0

DAVID BUTTON

BIRTHDATE:	27 February 1989
POSITION:	Goalkeeper
HEIGHT:	1.91m
OTHER CLUBS:	Tottenham Hotspur, Grays, Rochdale, Bournemouth, Luton, Dagenham & Redbridge, Crewe Alexandra, Shrewsbury Town, Plymouth, Leyton Orient, Doncaster Rovers, Barnsley, Charlton Athletic, Brentford, Fulham, Brighton
ALBION GAMES:	4
ALBION GOALS:	0

CONOR TOWNSEND

BIRTHDATE:	4 March 1993
POSITION:	Left-back
HEIGHT:	1.68m
OTHER CLUBS:	Hull, Grimsby, Chesterfield, Carlisle, Dundee United, Scunthorpe
ALBION GAMES:	65+10
ALBION GOALS:	1

DARA O'SHEA

BIRTHDATE:	4 March 1999
POSITION:	Defender
HEIGHT:	1.85m
OTHER CLUBS:	Exeter City (loan) Hereford (loan)
ALBION GAMES:	46+6
ALBION GOALS:	3

KYLE BARTLEY

BIRTHDATE:	22 May 1991
POSITION:	Centre-half
HEIGHT:	1.85m
OTHER CLUBS:	Arsenal, Sheffield United, Rangers, Swansea, Birmingham City, Leeds
ALBION GAMES:	89+7
ALBION GOALS:	7

SEMI AJAYI

BIRTHDATE:	9 November 1993
POSITION:	Centre-half
HEIGHT:	1.93m
OTHER CLUBS:	Charlton Athletic, Arsenal, Cardiff City, Rotherham United
ALBION GAMES:	76+3
ALBION GOALS:	8

MATT CLARKE

BIRTHDATE:	22 September 1996
POSITION:	Centre-half
HEIGHT:	1.85m
OTHER CLUBS:	Ipswich Town Portsmouth, Brighton
ALBION GAMES:	0
ALBION GOALS:	0

CEDRIC KIPRÉ

BIRTHDATE:	9 December 1996
POSITION:	Centre-half
HEIGHT:	1.93m
OTHER CLUBS:	Leicester City, Corby, Motherwell, Wigan Athletic, Charleroi
ALBION GAMES:	2+1
ALBION GOALS:	0

DARNELL FURLONG

BIRTHDATE:	31 October 1995
POSITION:	Right-back
HEIGHT:	1.80m
OTHER CLUBS:	QPR
ALBION GAMES:	56+13
ALBION GOALS:	3

JAKE LIVERMORE

BIRTHDATE:	14 November 1989
POSITION:	Midfielder
HEIGHT:	1.80m
OTHER CLUBS:	Tottenham Hotspur, Hull City
ALBION GAMES:	142+15
ALBION GOALS:	7

ALEX MOWATT

BIRTHDATE:	13 February 1995
POSITION:	Midfielder
HEIGHT:	1.73m
OTHER CLUBS:	Leeds United, Barnsley, Oxford United
ALBION GAMES:	0
ALBION GOALS:	0

55

ROBERT SNODGRASS

BIRTHDATE:	7 September 1987
POSITION:	Midfielder
HEIGHT:	1.83m
OTHER CLUBS:	Livingston, Stirling, Leeds United, Norwich City, Hull City, West Ham United, Aston Villa
ALBION GAMES:	6+2
ALBION GOALS:	0

QUEVIN CASTRO

BIRTHDATE:	16 August 2001
POSITION:	Midfielder
HEIGHT:	1.93m
OTHER CLUBS:	Thetford Town, Bury Town
ALBION GAMES:	0
ALBION GOALS:	0

GRADY DIANGANA

BIRTHDATE:	19 April 1998
POSITION:	Midfielder
HEIGHT:	1.80m
OTHER CLUBS:	West Ham United
ALBION GAMES:	39+13
ALBION GOALS:	9

MATT PHILLIPS

BIRTHDATE:	8 May 1998
POSITION:	Winger
HEIGHT:	1.85m
OTHER CLUBS:	Wycombe, Blackpool, QPR
ALBION GAMES:	132+40
ALBION GOALS:	23

ADAM REACH

BIRTHDATE:	3 February 1993
POSITION:	Winger
HEIGHT:	1.85m
OTHER CLUBS:	Middlesbrough, Darlington, Shrewsbury Town, Bradford City, Preston North End, Sheffield Wednesday
ALBION GAMES:	0
ALBION GOALS:	0

KENNETH ZOHORE

BIRTHDATE:	31 January 1994
POSITION:	Striker
HEIGHT:	1.89m
OTHER CLUBS:	Copenhagen, Fiorentina, OB, KV Kortrijk, Cardiff City
ALBION GAMES:	6+14
ALBION GOALS:	5

CALLUM ROBINSON

BIRTHDATE:	2 February 1995
POSITION:	Striker
HEIGHT:	1.78m
OTHER CLUBS:	Aston Villa, Preston North End, Bristol City, Sheffield United
ALBION GAMES:	30+15
ALBION GOALS:	9

KARLAN GRANT

BIRTHDATE:	18 September 1997
POSITION:	Striker
HEIGHT:	1.83m
OTHER CLUBS:	Charlton Athletic, Cambridge United, Crawley, Huddersfield Town
ALBION GAMES:	14+7
ALBION GOALS:	1

STATS CORRECT TO END OF 2020-21 SEASON

Matt Phillips

WHERE'S BAGGIE BIRD?

Quiz Answers

Page 20
Maze

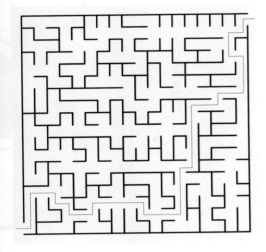

Page 25
Wordsearch

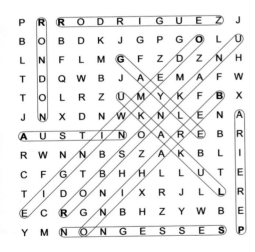

Page 38
Spot the ball!

Page 42
Crossword

01. LUKAKU
02. NAVY BLUE
03. VALERIAN
04. FIVE
05. TONY BROWN
06. THE HAWTHORNS
07. GRADY
08. THROSTLE
09. WILLIAMS
10. ALEX MOWATT
11. SAWYERS

Pages 46-47
The Big Quiz

1. Brighton & Hove Albion
2. Inter Miami
3. Seven
4. Republic of Ireland
5. France
6. Grady Diangana v Everton
7. Hal Robson-Kanu v Leeds United
8. Ben Foster
9. Two – Bobby Robson & Sam Allardyce
10. 1968
11. DOS Utrecht
12. Grasshoppers Zurich
13. West Bromwich Strollers
14. 172
15. Huddersfield Town
16. Stoney Lane
17. Blackpool
18. Aston Villa
19. True
20. Tony Brown

Page 50
Crossword

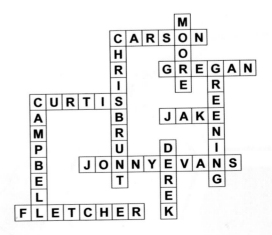

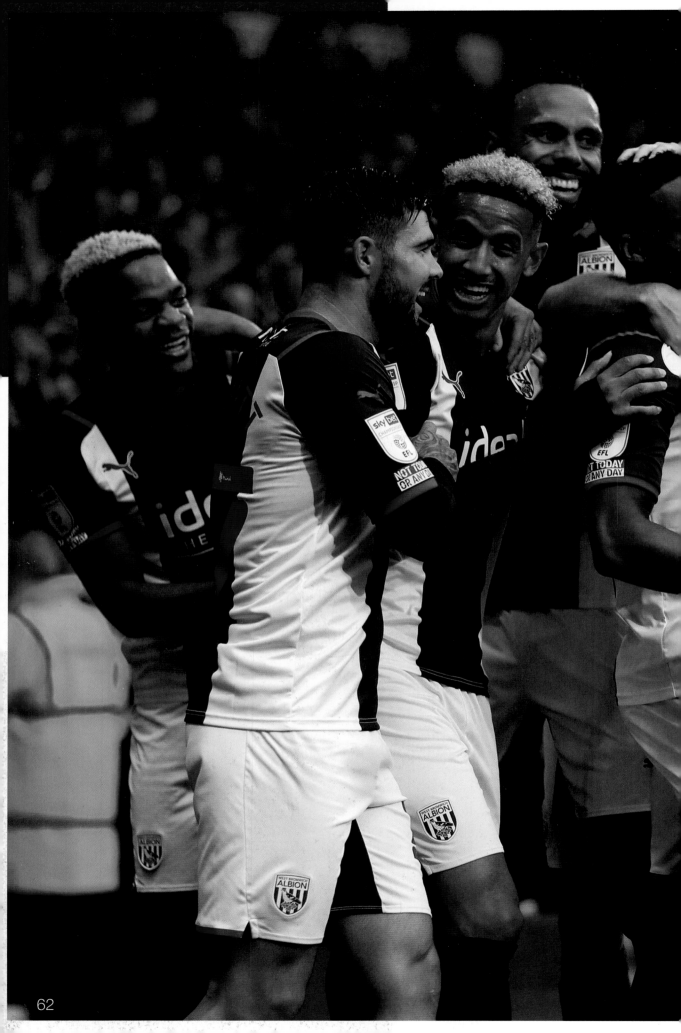